Manage Your Content and Devices
How to Archive, Gift, Lend, Borrow, and Delete Kindle Books
By Emery H. Maxwell

Table of Contents

Welcome

Welcome to the *Manage Your Content and Devices* guide. This manual is intended to help you understand and manage the different features of the *Kindle* device, focusing primarily on how to archive, gift, and delete *Kindle* books.

Using the *Kindle* device might be simple, but not everything about it is entirely intuitive. In fact, trying to figure it out by yourself can be overwhelming, especially if you have never owned a tablet before.

This is where a guide can be very useful.

It will cover:

• How to deliver content to your *Kindle* or *Kindle Fire*

• How to download content that is stored in the *Cloud*

• How to sort your content

• How to add or remove items from *Kindle*

• How to transfer content from your old *Kindle* to your new one

• How to lend or borrow *Kindle* Books

• How to share *Kindle* books with family members

• How to send and redeem a *Kindle* book to someone as a gift, or exchange it for an *Amazon* Gift Card

• Troubleshooting

• . . . and more.

It's time to get started.

How to Deliver Content to Your *Kindle or Kindle Fire*

Delivering items from the **Manage Your Content and Devices** page to your device or *Kindle* reading app can be done from your computer.

    1.) Make sure you are on your computer (not the *Kindle* tablet), and from there, go to the *Amazon* website and sign in.

    2.) Once you are signed in to your account, look toward the top of the screen on the *Amazon* web page and hold the cursor on **Account & Lists**.

    3.) A drop-down menu should appear. Scroll down and select **Your Content and Devices**.

    4.) You should now be on the **Manage Your Content and Devices** page. Select the title you'd like to deliver. Then click the **Actions** tab.

    5.) In the **Actions** tab, look to the right of where it says, "Deliver to," and select **Default Device** or **Others**.

    6.) Select **Deliver**. If you select **Others**, select the device(s) or *Kindle* reading app(s) from the drop-down menu, then click **Deliver**.

    Note: If the name of a device is faded, it is likely because the title you've selected is not compatible with it.

    Note: If you'd like to view titles that have not been sent to your device or reading app, you have the option to go to the **Show** menu (located on the left portion of the screen) and select **Pending Deliveries**.

<u>Understanding Device and *Cloud* Storage</u>

T he *Cloud* securely stores content that is purchased from the *Kindle* Store, including copies of all your books and recent issues of newspapers and magazines.

Cloud content can be accessed by tapping **Cloud** in the top-left corner of the Home screen or **All** in the top-left portion of the library screen.

Your documents are saved in the *Cloud* if they have been emailed to your *Kindle* and if you have enabled **Personal Document Archiving** in the **Manage Your Content and Devices** section.

If you'd like to view content that is stored on your *Kindle*, tap **On Device**.

Tip: If you plan to go offline and would still like to view content, tap **Cloud** and download any content to your *Kindle* that you'd like to have available.

Downloaded items can be opened from the Home screen or from the *Cloud*.

<u>How to Download Content that is Stored in the *Cloud*</u>

1.) Tap *Cloud* in the top-left corner of the Home screen.

2.) Tap on the items you'd like to download to your *Kindle*.

Tip: The download can be canceled by tapping on the item's title.

How to Manage your Content

The *Kindle* is capable of storing thousands of books, documents, newspapers, blogs, and magazines.

This list of content can be displayed by tapping the **Home** button, then selecting the **On Device** option.

View how much free space your *Kindle* has for storing content

1.) Tap the **Menu** button.

2.) Select **Settings**.

3.) On the **Settings** page, go to the menu and select **Device Info**.

Change the appearance of the *Home* screen

1.) Tap the **Menu** button.

2.) Select **List** or **Cover View**.

How to Sort your Content

By default, the content is sorted by Recent, which brings new items and the content you are currently reading to the top.

But there is a way to change the sort option.

1.) Make sure you are on the Home screen.

2.) Tap the name of the existing sort order, located under the toolbar.

Items that are stored in the *Cloud* can also be sorted.

Filter the content by type

1.) Go to the Home screen.

2.) Tap **All Items**, located under the toolbar.

How to Remove Items from *Kindle*

1.) Go to the Home screen.

2.) Press and hold the item's name or cover.

3.) Wait for the dialog box to pop up, then tap **Remove from Device**.

Note: This will not remove content from the *Cloud*. The content will securely remain in the *Cloud*, where it will be available to download at another time.

How to Transfer Content from an Old Kindle to your New One

Although most content is securely stored in the *Amazon Cloud*, there are certain documents that might need to be transferred manually.

Personal content that was transferred directly to your old *Kindle,* but was not emailed to it will need to undergo a different transfer procedure.

Download content to your new *Kindle* from the *Cloud* directly

1.) Go to the Home screen.

2.) Tap **My Library** in the top-left portion of the screen.

3.) You should now be at the library page. Tap **All** in the top-left portion of the screen.

Download personal content that was stored on your *Kindle*, but not emailed to it

1.) Using the USB cable, connect your *Kindle* device to a computer.

2.) Transfer the files or folders to the documents folder.

For more information about using the USB, refer to the *How to get more out of your reading experience* chapter and look under the *Connecting the Kindle device to a computer* section.

Cloud Collection

Cloud Collections allow you to organize the content on your device into customized categories that are stored in the Cloud.

The collections are synced between other devices that are registered to the same *Amazon* account and that support Cloud Collections. Items can be added to more than one collection.

How to Create a New Cloud Collection (6th Generation and newer)

1.) Go to the Home screen and tap the **Menu** button.

2.) Select **Create New Collection**.

3.) Using the keyboard, enter a name for the collection.

4.) Tap **OK**.

5.) There should now be a visible list of items that can be added to a collection.

6.) Tap the checkbox next to an item to add it to the collection.

7.) When you're finished, tap **Done**.

How to Create a New Cloud Collection (Older Generations)

1.) Go to the **Collections** page, then tap the **Add** (plus sign) icon.

2.) Enter the collection name, then tap **Next**.

3.) Select the title(s) to add to your collection.

4.) Tap the titles you'd like to include in your collection, then tap **Add**.

Add or Remove Items in a Cloud Collection (Newer Generations)

1.) Make sure you are in a collection.

2.) Tap the menu button.

3.) Select **Add/Remove Items**.

Add or Remove Items in a Cloud Collection (Older Generations)

1.) To add to a collection, press and hold the title.

2.) Tap the checkbox next to each collection you'd like to add the item to.

3.) Tap **Add**.

How to Filter the Content on the Home Screen by Collection

1.) Tap **All Items** or the currently selected filter.

2.) Select **Collections**.

The collections you download to your device will be displayed in the **All Items, Books, Periodicals,** and **Docs** sections.

If you'd like to download a collection, simply press and hold the onscreen collection cover or title and tap **Add to Device**. This setting is device-sensitive, however, and it will not be saved if you decide to remove your device from registration.

If you'd like to remove a collection, press and hold the onscreen collection cover or title and tap **Remove from Device**.

Tip: Deleting a collection from your *Kindle* will not remove the content stored on your device or in the *Cloud*. Items previously placed into the collection that are stored on your *Kindle* will still appear on the Home screen and in the *Cloud*.

Deleting a collection that was created on a device or in a reading app that supports *Cloud Collections* will delete it from the *Cloud* and other devices or reading apps that support *Cloud Collections* and are registered to the same *Amazon* account.

Periodicals

Magazines and newspapers are kept in folders that are grouped by periodical name.

To free up space on your device, issues that are more than eight issues old, newspapers that are more than fourteen issues old, and magazines that are more than forty issues old will be deleted automatically.

However, there are two ways to keep a copy of an issue on your device.

<u>Option 1</u>

1.) Go to the Home screen.

2.) Tap **On Device**.

3.) Press and hold the onscreen name or cover of the issue you'd like to keep.

4.) Select **Keep This Issue**.

<u>Option 2</u>

1.) Go to the issue.

2.) Tap the **Menu** (icon with 3 dots) button.

3.) Select **Keep This Issue**.

How to Send and Redeem a *Kindle* Book as a Gift, or Exchange it for an *Amazon* Gift Card

*K*indle books can be sent and received as gifts by you even if you don't own a *Fire* tablet or *Kindle e-reader*, as long as the email addresses of the sender and recipients are valid.

The *Kindle* book gift can be read by the recipients on a supported *Amazon* device or reading app.

Purchasing and Sending the *Kindle Book as a Gift*

1.) If you haven't done so already, sign up for *Amazon's 1-Click payment* method. This can be accomplished by going to the **Manage Your Content and Devices** section, selecting the **Settings** tab, and then clicking **Edit Payment Method** below **Digital Payment Settings**.

2.) After you have verified that the payment method is in place, go to the *Kindle Store* in your desktop browser and select the book you'd like to purchase as a gift.

Note: Currently, free books, books on PRE-ORDER, and subscriptions cannot be gifted.

3.) On the book's detail page (sales page), select the **Give as a Gift** tab.

4.) Enter the email address of the person you'd like to send the gift to.

If you are unsure of the recipient's email address, select **Email the gift to me** before placing your order. This will allow you to forward the gift email or print and personally deliver it to the recipient. After the recipient logs in to his or her *Amazon* account, he or she can enter the **Gift Claim Code** from the email.

5.) Enter a delivery date. You can also enter a gift message, but this is optional.

6.) Click **Place your order** to complete the process.

Tip: It is possible to redeliver a *Kindle* book gift you've purchased. Simply go to **Your Digital Orders** in the **Your Account** section. From the order summary page, click the **Resend E-mail** tab.

Note: The availability of certain titles may vary by country and copyright restrictions. If a title isn't available for your gift recipient, have the recipient contact *Amazon* and they will exchange the gift for an *Amazon Gift Card* of equal value.

How to Redeem a *Kindle* Book as a Gift

Kindle books can be received as gifts even if the recipient does not own a *Fire* tablet or *Kindle* e-reader. If the recipient does not have a supported *Amazon* device registered to his or her account, he or she can download a free *Kindle* reading app after the gift is received.

1.) Click **Get your *Kindle* Book Gift Now** from the gift notification email. This will allow the recipient to view their gift on *Amazon*.

2.) Click **Accept your *Kindle* Book Gift**. Log in to your *Amazon* account if you are prompted to do so.

If you have received a *Kindle* book gift at an email address that isn't connected to your *Fire* tablet, *Kindle* e-reader, or *Kindle* reading app, click **Use a different *Amazon* account**. Then sign in to the account where you would like to redeem the *Kindle* book.

3.) From the drop-down menu, select the *Kindle* e-reader, *Fire* tablet, or *Kindle* reading app that you would like the gift delivered to.

How to Exchange a *Kindle* Book for an *Amazon* Gift Card

1.) Open the gift email you received, then click the link to redeem your *Kindle* book gift.

2.) Enter the gift claim code in the box, then select the **Go get you gift!** Tab.

3.) On the **Accept your *Kindle* Book Gift** page, click **Learn how this works or exchange for gift credit**.

4.) On the next screen, click **Request your gift credit from customer service now**.

After completing these steps, the *Amazon* gift card will be applied to your *Amazon* account automatically.

How to Lend or Borrow *Kindle* Books

Y ou can lend a *Kindle* book to a friend or family member for up to 14 days. But the *Kindle* book must be loaned only one time.

Currently, magazines and newspapers are not available for lending.

Note: The person who loans the book to the recipient will not be able to read the book during the loan period.

How to Loan a *Kindle* Book from the Product Detail Page

1.) Go to the *Kindle* store from your computer.

2.) Locate the title you'd like to loan.

3.) On the book's detail page (sales page), select **Loan this book**.

4.) Enter the recipient's email address. You can also enter a message, but that's optional. The *Kindle* book's loan notification must be sent to the recipient's personal email address, not their *Send to Kindle* email address.

5.) Click **Send now**.

How to Loan a *Kindle* Book from *Manage Your Content and Devices*

1.) Go to **Manage Your Content and Devices**. If you are unsure how to get there, see steps 1 through 3 in the *How to Deliver Content to your Kindle or Kindle Fire* chapter.

2.) Select the **Actions** button for the title you'd like to loan.

3.) Select **Loan this title**.

Note: If **Loan this title** is not an option, lending is unavailable for that particular book.

4.) Enter the recipient's email address.

5.) Click **Send now**.

How to Borrow a *Kindle* Book from a Friend

When someone loans you a *Kindle* book, you will receive an email notification. That email will allow you to download the book to your supported *Kindle* reading app, *Fire* tablet, or *Kindle* e-reader.

1.) Open the email message that's titled "*A Loaned Book for You.*"

2.) Click the **Get your loaned book now** tab. Your web browser will launch automatically to the *Amazon* website, so you can accept the loan.

3.) Sign in to the *Amazon* account where you'd like to read the book.

• If you have a *Kindle* reading app, *Kindle* e-reader, or *Fire* tablet, select which device you would like the book to be delivered to. Then click **Accept loaned book.**

• If you do not have a *Kindle* reading app, *Kindle* e-reader, or *Fire* tablet, click **Accept loaned book** and follow the on-screen instructions to download a *Kindle* reading app for free.

How to Return a Loaned *Kindle* Book

1.) Go to the **Manage Your Content and Devices** section.

2.) Select the **Actions** button next to the borrowed book.

3.) Select **Delete from Library**.

4.) Click **Yes** to confirm.

How to Share Kindle Books with Family Members

Certain types of content that meet eligibility requirements can be shared with people in your *Amazon* household through the *Family Library*.

Before the *Family Library* can be used, you have to join the *Amazon* household together. *Amazon* household members include:

• Up to four children, as long as their profiles are created from an adult's account.

• Two adults, each with their own *Amazon* account.

• Up to four teen logins. However, **teens are unable to share content**.

* Some devices may need to be enabled before shared content can be viewed.

How to Create an *Amazon* Household

Creating an *Amazon* Household with a teen

1.) Go to your *Amazon* account.

2.) Go to *Amazon Household*.

3.) Select **Add a Teen**.

An email invitation will be sent to your teenager. The teen will need to accept the parent's email invitation to begin the setup process for login credentials.

Creating an *Amazon* Household with a child

1.) Go to your *Amazon* account.

2.) Go to *Amazon Household*.

3.) Select **Add a child**.

Creating an *Amazon* Household with another adult

1.) After going to your *Amazon* account, go to *Amazon Household*.

2.) Select **Add an Adult**.

3.) After entering the name and email address of the adult you'd like to send the invitation to, select **Continue**.

4.) You have the option to share *Prime* benefits and create a *Family Library*. If this is something you are interested in doing, select the option to share your wallet.

5.) Confirm the name and email address of the other adult, then select **Send Invite**.

* They will have 14 days to accept the invitation. To manage the invitation, go to *Manage Your Household*.

You can also create an *Amazon Household* with another adult by signing in together.

1.) After going to your *Amazon* account, go to *Amazon Household*, then select **Add an Adult**.

2.) Select **Have them sign in on this device**.

3.) The other adult will need to verify their existing account credentials or create a new account.

4.) If you'd like to share *Prime* benefits and create a *Family Library*, you have the option to do so by selecting the option to share your wallet.

5.) Select **Next** to create your *Amazon Household*.

How to Share Content through *Family Library*

1.) Go to **Manage Your Content and Devices**, then select **Your Content**.

2.) Select the **Show** drop-down menu, then choose the content type you'd like to share.

3.) Check the box next to the title you'd like to share.

4.) Select **Add to Library**.

* If you don't see **Add to Library** after you've selected a title, you may need to select **Show Family Library**.

5.) Select a profile from the drop-down menu, then click **OK**.

<u>Content that cannot be shared</u>

- *Prime Video*
- *Kindle Unlimited* titles
- Subscriptions
- Magazines and newspapers
- Music in your *Music Library*

<u>How to Permanently Delete *Kindle* Books and Personal Documents from Your Content Library</u>

P ermanently removing books from the **Manage Your Content and Devices** section will require you to download them again if you ever want to obtain them again in the future.

1.) Go to the **Manage Your Content and Devices** section. If you are unsure how to get there, refer to steps 1 through 3 in the *How to Deliver Content to Your Kindle or Kindle Fire* chapter.

2.) Under the **Your Content** heading, adjust the drop-down menu to the correct category if it's not in place already.

3.) Select the title(s) you'd like to delete, then select **Delete**.

4.) When it asks you for confirmation, select **Yes, delete permanently**.

Troubleshooting

Many issues, such as screen freezing, can be resolved by simply restarting the device.

How to restart the device

1.) Press and hold the power button for approximately seven seconds until the dialog box becomes displayed on the screen.

2.) Tap **Restart**.

If the device is so unresponsive that the dialog box does not appear, a forced restart is necessary. To perform a forced restart, press and hold the power button for approximately forty seconds until the device restarts.

Battery is not charging properly or is draining too rapidly

• Verify that you are using a compatible USB cable and that it is securely connected.

• If you are using a power adapter, verify that it is not faulty.

• Place the device into *Sleep* mode when you are finished reading.

• Power off the wireless connection to save power.

Can't connect to WI-FI

• Check the wireless connectivity on the *Kindle*.

• Verify that the wireless router is set to use a WI-FI channel from 1 to 11.

• Restart the modem or router by unplugging it and plugging it back in.

Can't remember pass-code

The device will need to be reset.

Important Note: Resetting the device will remove all of your personal information, including parental controls, your lock screen pass-code, *Amazon* account information, WI-FI settings, and downloaded content.

However, any content you have purchased from *Amazon* will remain securely stored in the *Cloud* and can be downloaded again after you register the *Kindle* to your account.

To reset the device:

1.) Bring up the onscreen keyboard by tapping the pass-code field.

2.) Type **111222777**, then tap **OK**.

You'll need to connect to a wireless network and register the device to use your *Kindle* again.

Content doesn't seem to download

• **Sync to receive the content**

1.) Go to the **Home** screen.

2.) Tap the **Menu** icon.

3.) Tap **Sync and Check for Items**.

• **Check wireless connection status**

1.) Go to the **Home** screen or any **Settings** screen.

• Make sure **Airplane** mode is not powered on.

• Verify that your device is running the latest software version.

• Verify that your payment method is valid.

• Check if you are filtering content on your Home screen. You can check by going to the Home page and selecting the **On Device** tab. Make sure it is displaying **All items**.

Content will not sync

• Check the wireless connection status.

• Make sure the device is running the latest software version.

• Verify that **WHISPERSYNC** for books is enabled on the *Kindle* device.

1.) Go to the Home screen.

2.) Tap the **Menu** icon.

3.) Go to **Settings**.

4.) Go to **Device Options**.

5.) Go to **Personalize Your *Kindle***

6.) Go to **Advanced Options**.

7.) Enable *WHISPERSYNC for Books* if it's not enabled already.

• Verify that **WHISPERSYNC Device Synchronization** is enabled on your *Amazon* account.

1.) Go to the *Amazon* web site from your computer.

2.) Go to the **Manage Your Content and Devices** section.

3.) Select **Settings**.

4.) Look under **Device Synchronization** and make sure that **WHISPERSYNC Device Synchronization** is on.

Book does not open

• Make sure that the device is connected to WI-FI.

• Remove the book, restart the device, and download the book again.

<u>More from Emery H. Maxwell</u>

Fire HD 10 Tablet Manual, available at all *Amazon* stores, including <u>U.S.</u> and <u>U.K.</u>

Fire HD 8 Manual User Guide, available at all *Amazon* stores, including <u>U.S.</u> and <u>U.K.</u>

For even more books, simply visit the *Emery H. Maxwell* author page, available at all *Amazon* stores, including <u>U.S.</u>

Thank you for purchasing *Manage Your Content and Devices*.